Let's Get Crafty with Salt-Dough

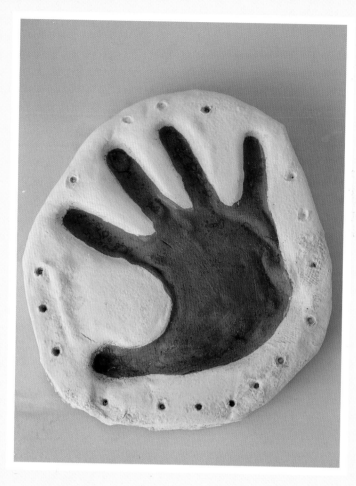

Let's Get Crafty
with
Salt-Dough

FOR KIDS AGED 2 AND UP

CICO **Kidz**

Published in 2016 by CICO Books
An imprint of Ryland Peters & Small Ltd
20–21 Jockey's Fields   341 E 116th St
London WC1R 4BW   New York, NY 10029

www.rylandpeters.com

10 9 8 7 6 5 4 3 2 1

A CIP catalog record for this book is available from the
Library of Congress and the British Library.

ISBN: 978 1 78249 384 6

Printed in China

Editor: Katie Hardwicke
Designer: Eoghan O'Brien
Photographer: Terry Benson
Stylist: Emily Breen

In-house editor: Dawn Bates
In-house designer: Fahema Khanam
Art director: Sally Powell
Production controller: David Hearn
Publishing manager: Penny Craig
Publisher: Cindy Richards

For additional photography credits, see page 79.

Contents

Introduction	6
What you will need	8
Making salt-dough	10
Salt-dough tips	13
Donuts	14
Stamped Magnets	16
Twinkly Stars	19
Fluffy Sheep	22
Patterned Tiles	24
What's the Weather Today?	26
Sheriff's Badge	28
Teddy's Tea Set	31
Softy the Snowman	34
Gingerbread Family	37
Brilliant Beads	40
Tic Tac Toe	42
Little Ladybug	46
Fairy Toadstools	49
Pretty Flower Brooch	52
Fun Fruit	54
Handprint Tile	58
Dotty Dino	60
Trinket Pot	62
Hanging Butterflies	64
Fishing Game	67
Springtime Eggs	70
Lovely Letters	72
Cute Caterpillar	74
Pretty Pendant	77
Suppliers	79
Index	80

Introduction

KNEADING, ROLLING, MOLDING, AND SHAPING ARE ALL ACTIVITIES ENJOYED BY YOUNG CHILDREN, AND SALT-DOUGH IS THE IDEAL CRAFT ACTIVITY TO INDULGE THEIR NEWFOUND SKILLS. MADE FROM BASIC INGREDIENTS THAT YOU WILL FIND IN YOUR KITCHEN CABINET, THE FUN STARTS WITH MIXING THE SALT-DOUGH ITSELF, PRODUCING A SMOOTH AND TACTILE DOUGH THAT IS INCREDIBLY FORGIVING AND ADAPTABLE. MOLD AND SHAPE IT, OR CUT OUT SHAPES WITH COOKIE CUTTERS, THEN BAKE AND FINISH WITH PAINT AND AN ASSORTMENT OF DECORATIONS FROM YOUR CRAFT STASH.

Getting crafty with salt-dough is the ideal activity for rainy afternoons, mid-morning lulls, play dates, and party planning, and in this book you'll find plenty of ideas and inspiration for fun craft activities that you can make together.

The salt-dough projects in this book range from pretty jewelry—try the flower brooch on page 52, the heart pendant on page 77, or the beads on page 40—through to room decorations like the hanging butterflies on page 64 or the letters on page 72. You'll find lots of ideas on what do with your creations, with plenty of games that will appeal to little ones—they'll love hooking the fish on page 67, trying the memory game on page 24, or mastering the game on page 42. Making models from salt-dough is exciting, too—start with the cute fluffy sheep on page 22, then add a snowman (page 34) or caterpillar (page 74), or try your hand at the fabulous rainbow on page 26. For playtime fun there's nothing like making your own play food and you'll find ideas for fruit (page 54) and donuts (page 14) that are sure to inspire more homemade groceries.

 All the actions involved in modeling salt-dough are great ways for young children to develop fine motor skills and coordination. While many projects will only need light adult supervision, there are some steps that will require your help. We have marked these with a helping hands symbol as a guide. Working as a team is all part of the fun and your child will enjoy spending time with you and learning from you, as you get crafty together.

WHAT YOU WILL NEED

For all the projects you will need some basic craft materials. Keep a dedicated corner or drawer for storing your equipment, and stock up on a few craft items for the finishing touches—a good supply of googly eyes is essential! Making salt-dough is a fun activity in itself but decorating the baked projects with paint, gems, feathers, pompoms, ribbons, or other pieces from your craft stash will transform them into unique creations to treasure.

BASIC SALT-DOUGH EQUIPMENT

- Measuring cup
- Measuring spoons
- Mixing bowl and wooden spoon
- Rolling pin
- Baking sheet or microwaveable plate
- Non-stick baking parchment
- Plastic wrap/clingfilm
- Cookie cutters
- Wooden skewer
- Plastic drinking straws

CRAFT ESSENTIALS

- Glitter
- Sequins, gems, and beads
- Wooden shapes
- Feathers
- Pompoms
- Yarn
- Buttons, ribbons, and braid
- Felt and fabric
- Pipe cleaners
- Googly eyes

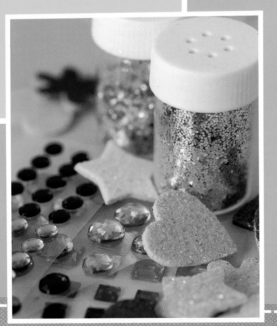

BASIC SUPPLIES

- Water-based paints and paintbrushes
- Felt-tipped pens or marker pens
- White/PVA glue and spreader or brush
- Sticky tape
- Pencils, ruler, and eraser
- Craft scissors
- Paper plates
- Paper towels
- Plastic containers

GETTING MESSY!

Much of the fun of crafting is the chance to get messy, and to make some mess! Follow these tips before you begin for stress-free crafting:

- Cover your work table with newspaper or a wipe-down sheet or tablecloth
- Protect your child's clothes with an apron or old t-shirt (you may want to do the same!)
- Roll up sleeves and tie long hair out of the way
- Keep a roll of paper towels close by
- When using glitter or sprinkles, put a sheet of paper or newspaper beneath the project and use it to pour the excess glitter back into the pot afterward

CLEARING UP!

Ask your child to help to clear up afterward—washing up paintbrushes and pots will appeal to all those who love to play with water!

- Wash up mixing bowls, spoons, and cookie cutters, and wipe down surfaces
- Put all lids back on glue pots, paint pots and tubes, and felt-tipped pens
- Wash paintbrushes and palettes; stand paintbrushes in a jar to dry
- Put any equipment away in drawers or boxes to keep it organized and easy to find next time

MAKING SALT-DOUGH

Mix up a batch of dough following the recipe, which is sufficient to make the projects in the book.

1

Measure out the salt, flour, and lukewarm water. Put the salt in a mixing bowl and add the flour. Stir together.

Gradually add the water to the dough, mixing with your hands or a wooden spoon, until the dough comes together in a ball.

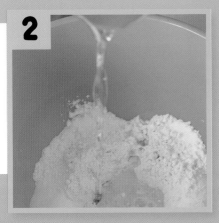

2

Knead the mixture in the bowl, or on your work surface, with your hands to form a smooth, firm dough. Add a little more water if the dough is too dry, or more flour if it is too sticky.

3

MAKING COLORED SALT-DOUGH

You can color your dough before baking by simply diluting paint in the water and stirring it in as you make the dough. Food coloring can also be used, and produces pretty pastel shades.

Measure out your ingredients as opposite. Stir your paint into the measured water to get the intensity of color that you require.

Make the dough following the instructions above, adding the colored water as normal in Step 2.

BAKING SALT-DOUGH OVEN METHOD

1 Preheat the oven to its lowest setting, approximately 210°F/100°C/Gas ½.

2 Put your salt-dough pieces or models on a baking sheet lined with non-stick baking parchment and bake in the oven for an hour, or until they are completely hard. Large or solid pieces may take longer.

3 Leave the baking sheet in the oven to cool and prevent the salt-dough shapes from cracking.

BAKING SALT-DOUGH MICROWAVE METHOD

1 Once prepared, put your salt-dough pieces or models on a microwaveable plate on a piece of baking parchment.

2 Microwave on high for bursts of 30 seconds until the dough is baked and hard.

MAKING VARNISH

To add a shine to your salt-dough creations and make them hard-wearing, you can mix up a varnish from white/PVA glue and water.

Use a clean plastic pot, like a yogurt pot, to mix the glue. Measure out two parts glue to one part water, and stir them together.

Once your baked salt-dough has been painted and is dry, use a clean paintbrush to apply the varnish. Let it dry—it will dry clear and shiny.

SALT-DOUGH TIPS

Sprinkle your work surface with flour to prevent the dough from sticking when you roll it out.

Unbaked salt-dough binds together well, but you can use a little water to help pieces stick together if required.

The edge of a ruler makes a safe "knife" for cutting dough.

When using cookie cutters, leave the cutter in the dough and peel the excess dough away from the cutter to help retain the shape.

Dip cookie cutters in flour before cutting out shapes from the dough.

Wrap any unused salt-dough in plastic wrap/clingfilm to prevent it from drying out.

Insert short lengths of drinking straws to keep holes open when baking.

Donuts

THE BAKERY IS A GREAT SOURCE OF INSPIRATION FOR SALT-DOUGH CREATIONS! THESE DONUTS ARE SO EASY TO MAKE, WITH LOTS OF FUN TO BE HAD CHOOSING THE FROSTING COLOR AND ADDING THE SPRINKLE—TRY BEADS, SEQUINS, GLITTER, OR SIMPLY LEAVE THEM PLAIN WITH A GLAZE OF VARNISH TO GIVE THEM AN AUTHENTIC SHEEN.

WHAT YOU WILL NEED

- Basic salt-dough recipe (see page 10)
- Basic equipment (see page 8)
- Water-based paints and paintbrush
- White/PVA glue
- Seed beads, buttons, beads, sequins

1 **MAKE THE SALT-DOUGH** Follow the recipe on page 10 to make a quantity of salt-dough, kneading it to form a ball.

2 **ROLL OUT** Sprinkle flour onto the work surface. Take a large piece of dough and roll it into a thick, long sausage.

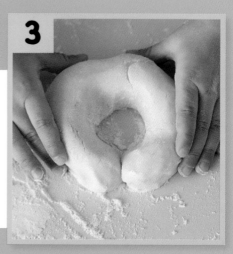

3 **MAKE A RING** Curve the sausage shape around to join the two ends, making a donut shape. Mold the ends together. Put the donut on the baking sheet or microwaveable plate and make a few more.

4 **[hand icon]** **BAKE** Bake the donuts following the instructions on pages 11–12 until completely hard. Let cool.

ADD FROSTING Choose your frosting color and paint the top of the donut shape and about halfway down the sides.

ADD SPRINKLES If you want to decorate your donut with sprinkles, add them while the paint is still wet. Scatter over some tiny seed beads or sequins, then let dry. You can also glue buttons and larger beads to the donut when it is dry.

Tip

CAUTION: Your donuts may look very life-like so make sure your little one doesn't try to take a bite!

To give your donuts a sheen, and make them more hard-wearing, paint a layer of varnish over them when they are dry. See page 12 for how to make a varnish from glue.

Stamped Magnets

DISPLAYING YOUR CHILD'S CREATIONS IS A GREAT WAY OF ENCOURAGING CREATIVITY AND THIS PROJECT TICKS ALL THE BOXES. ONCE YOU'VE MADE THE MAGNETS, YOU CAN USE THEM TO ATTACH YOUR CHILD'S ARTWORKS TO THE FRIDGE FOR ALL TO SEE!

WHAT YOU WILL NEED

- White/PVA glue
- Cotton spool (reel)
- Flower button
- Basic salt-dough recipe (see page 10)
- Basic equipment (see page 8)
- Round cookie cutters
- Water-based paints and paintbrush
- Small magnet

1

MAKE STAMP Put a dab of glue on top of the spool (reel) and stick the flower button in place so that the patterned side is facing up. Let dry completely.

2 **MAKE THE SALT-DOUGH** Follow the recipe on page 10 to make a quantity of salt-dough, kneading it to form a ball.

ROLL OUT THE DOUGH Sprinkle flour onto the work surface and place the ball of dough on top. Roll the dough out with a rolling pin to an even thickness of about ½in. (1cm).

CUT OUT CIRCLES Using round cookie cutters, cut circles from the dough that are a little larger than the diameter of your spool and button.

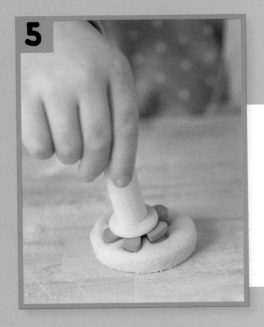

STAMP PATTERN Use the stamp to imprint the flower pattern on the circles—don't press too hard or the pattern will distort. Place on the baking sheet or microwaveable plate. Stamp a few more shapes.

6 **BAKE** Bake the stamped circles following the instructions on pages 11–12, until completely hard. Let cool.

7

PAINT When the patterned circles are hard and dry, paint them in your chosen colors, painting them on all sides. Let dry. To give the magnets a sheen, add a little varnish (see page 12).

8

ATTACH MAGNET Add a generous amount of glue to the back of the dried circle and stick a magnet in place. Let dry. Your magnets are ready to adorn your fridge!

Twinkly Stars

THESE SPARKLY STARS MAKE THE PERFECT HOMEMADE CHRISTMAS DECORATIONS AND WILL KEEP CHILDREN HAPPILY OCCUPIED WITH CUTTING OUT, PAINTING, AND GLUING IN THE RUN UP TO THE FESTIVE SEASON. THEY ALSO MAKE GREAT ROOM DECORATIONS FOR THOSE WHO LIKE TO STARGAZE.

WHAT YOU WILL NEED

- Basic salt-dough recipe (see page 10)
- Basic equipment (see page 8)
- Star cookie cutters
- Wooden skewer (optional)
- Short drinking straw (optional)
- Water-based paints and paintbrush
- White/PVA glue
- Glitter, gems, sequins
- Ribbon

1 **MAKE THE SALT-DOUGH** Follow the recipe on page 10 to make a quantity of salt-dough, kneading it to form a ball.

2

ROLL OUT THE DOUGH Sprinkle flour onto the work surface and place the ball of dough on top. Roll the dough out with a rolling pin to an even thickness of about ½in. (1cm).

3

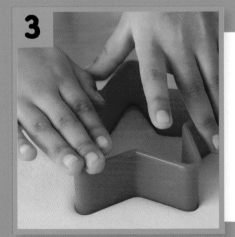

CUT OUT Using the cookie cutter, cut out the star shapes from the dough and put them on the baking sheet. Re-roll the dough and cut out as many stars as required.

ADD HOLE If you would like to hang your stars, make a hole through the dough using a wooden skewer or the end of a paintbrush. Make sure the hole is large enough to thread through the ribbon or twine. To keep the hole open while baking, use a drinking straw (see page 13)

5 **BAKE** Bake the stars following the instructions on pages 11–12 until completely hard. Let cool.

PAINT When your stars are completely dry, paint them a bright yellow. Make sure that you cover the whole surface of the star, including the back. Let dry.

DECORATE To make your stars sparkle and shine, add dots of glue and sprinkle with glitter, or add shiny gems and sequins. The sparklier the better!

8

THREAD RIBBON To hang the star, thread a length of ribbon through the hole and tie the ends in a knot.

Fluffy Sheep

THIS LITTLE SHEEP IS SO CUTE, AND LOOKS AS FLUFFY AS COTTON BALLS! IT WILL BE HARD TO STOP AT MAKING JUST ONE, AND BEFORE LONG YOU CAN HAVE A WHOLE FLOCK, EACH ONE A LITTLE DIFFERENT, WITH SOME GORGEOUS LITTLE LAMBS TOO.

WHAT YOU WILL NEED

- Basic salt-dough recipe (see page 10)
- Basic equipment (see page 8)
- Water-based paints and paintbrush
- White/PVA glue
- Googly eyes

1 **MAKE THE SALT-DOUGH** Follow the recipe on page 10 to make a quantity of salt-dough, kneading it to form a ball.

MAKE THE FEET Take four small pieces of dough and roll them into balls between your hands. Flatten the balls slightly to make the feet and put them on the baking sheet or microwaveable plate.

ROLL BALLS The body is made up of lots of small balls of dough. Take a little dough and roll it into a ball, then keep going until you have about 20 balls. Join the balls together to make a round body shape.

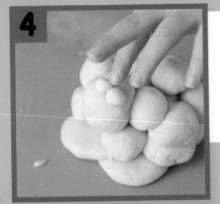

4

ADD THE HEAD Roll a slightly larger ball for the head and add it to the body. Now add the ears, using two very small balls of dough.

5 **BAKE** Bake your sheep following the instructions on pages 11–12 until completely hard. Let cool.

6

PAINT SHEEP Start by painting the body white, then paint the head, ears, and feet black. Let the paint dry completely. Use a dab of glue to add the googly eyes to the head.

Crafty Tip

Turn your sheep into a rare breed by using different color paints for the fleece.

Patterned Tiles

THIS PROJECT HELPS CHILDREN TO LEARN ABOUT PATTERNS AND IF YOU MAKE MATCHING PAIRS OF TILES IT CAN BE MADE INTO A FUN MEMORY GAME. TO PLAY THE GAME, PLACE THE TILES FACE DOWN AND TAKE IT IN TURNS TO TURN THEM OVER TO FIND MATCHING PAIRS. THE KEY IS TO REMEMBER WHERE THE TILES ARE!

WHAT YOU WILL NEED

- Basic salt-dough recipe (see page 10)
- Basic equipment (see page 8)
- Ruler
- Wooden skewer
- Water-based paint and paintbrush
- White/PVA glue (optional)
- Glitter and gems (optional)

1 **MAKE THE SALT-DOUGH** Follow the recipe on page 10 to make a quantity of salt-dough, kneading it to form a ball.

2

ROLL OUT THE DOUGH Sprinkle flour onto the work surface and place the ball of dough on top. Roll the dough out with a rolling pin to an even thickness of about ½in. (1cm).

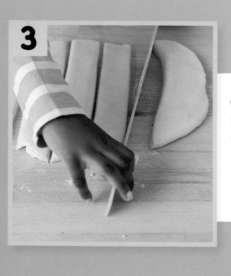

3

CUT OUT TILES Use the side of a ruler to cut the dough into horizontal strips about 1¼in. (3cm) wide. Now cut vertical strips to divide the dough into rectangles. Make as many as you can from the rolled dough.

SCORE PATTERNS Use a wooden skewer or the end of a paintbrush to draw patterns into the tiles—make dots, straight lines, grids, wavy lines, circles. If you are making a memory pairs game, repeat the patterns on pairs of tiles.

5 **BAKE** Place the tiles on a baking sheet or microwaveable plate. Bake following the instructions on pages 11–12 until completely hard. Let cool.

PAINT Paint the front of the tiles in lots of colors. For a pairs game, make sure you paint the matching pairs in the same color. You can also glue on even more decoration with glitter and gems, if you like.

What's the Weather Today?

BECOME A WEATHER REPORTER WITH THESE COLORFUL SYMBOLS THAT MAKE AN IDEAL STARTING PLACE FOR DISCUSSING THE EVERYDAY WORLD. WE'VE MADE A RAINBOW, SUN, AND RAIN CLOUD WITH COLORED DOUGH (SEE PAGE 11), BUT YOU COULD EXTEND THE ACTIVITY WITH RAINDROPS, A LIGHTNING BOLT, AND SNOWFLAKES.

WHAT YOU WILL NEED

- Basic salt-dough recipe (see page 10)
- Basic equipment (see page 8)
- Water-based paints and paintbrush
- Ruler

TO MAKE THE RAINBOW

COLOR THE SALT-DOUGH Follow the recipe on page 10 to make a quantity of salt-dough, kneading it to form a ball. Separate the dough into seven pieces and follow the instructions on page 11 to color the dough with different rainbow colors: red, orange, yellow, green, light blue, blue, and purple.

ROLL OUT Roll each ball of colored dough into a long, thin sausage shape. Try to keep the rolls the same size and length. Place them together in order—red, orange, yellow, green, pale blue, blue, and purple—as you go.

3

CURVE THE SHAPE When all the colored rolls are prepared, squeeze them together in order, then bend the shape to curve it into a rainbow.

4

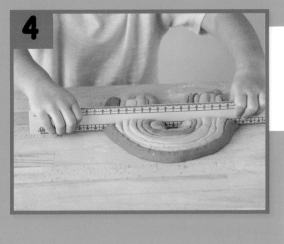

TRIM EDGES Use the side of a ruler to trim the bottom of the rainbow.

5 **BAKE** Place the shapes on a baking sheet or microwaveable plate and bake following the instructions on pages 11–12 until completely hard. Let cool.

TO MAKE A SUN AND CLOUD

MAKE MORE WEATHER! You can make more weather symbols by simply modeling the dough. Use the pale blue dough to roll small balls, then press them together to make a rain cloud. Use the yellow and orange dough to make a sun, with a round ball in the center and rays of rolled dough around the edge.

6

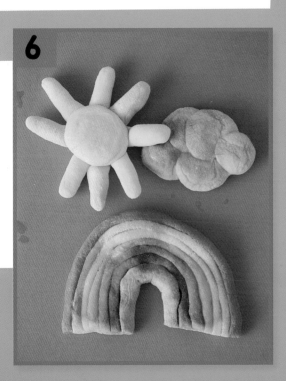

Sheriff's Badge

THIS SHERIFF'S BADGE IS SURE TO GO DOWN WELL WITH WILD WEST FANS. MADE WITH A COOKIE CUTTER STAR, YOUNG CHILDREN WILL LOVE PRESSING OUT SHAPES FROM THE DOUGH TO CREATE THEIR PERSONALIZED BADGE. PAINT AND DECORATE THEM WITH A BUTTON OR BEAD. THEN GLUE A BROOCH PIN TO THE BACK. THIS IDEA CAN BE ADAPTED WITH FLOWER CUTTERS TO MAKE A PRETTY BROOCH (SEE PAGE 52).

WHAT YOU WILL NEED

- Basic salt-dough recipe (see page 10)
- Basic equipment (see page 8)
- Star and round cookie cutters
- Water-based paints and paintbrush
- White/PVA glue
- Button
- Brooch pin

1

MAKE THE SALT-DOUGH Follow the recipe on page 10 to make a quantity of salt-dough, mixing it to form a firm dough.

2

ROLL OUT THE DOUGH Sprinkle some flour onto the work surface and roll out the dough to a thickness of about ¼in. (5mm) using the rolling pin.

3 CUT OUT THE STAR Using the shaped cookie cutters, cut out a star shape and a small inner circle.

ADD STAR POINTS Roll small blobs of dough and add to the points of the star.

5 BAKE Place the shapes on a baking sheet or microwaveable plate and bake following the instructions on pages 11–12 until completely hard. Let cool.

6 PAINT Paint the pieces in bright colors, making sure you have covered the sides, front and back thoroughly, and let them dry.

7

ADD BROOCH PIN Using a dab of white/PVA glue, stick the brooch pin to the back of the badge. Let it dry.

GLUE TOGETHER Using a dab of glue, stick the painted inner circle to the middle of the star and then glue a button onto the center. Let them dry. If you want to give your badge a shiny look, paint it with a little varnish (see page 12).

8

Crafty Tip

If you don't have a brooch pin, use a safety pin instead—see page 53 for how to attach it to the badge.

Teddy's Tea Set

MOLDING SOLID SHAPES IN SALT-DOUGH IS GREAT FUN. THERE'S PLENTY TO DO FOR THIS TEA SET—ROLLING HANDLES, SHAPING SPOUTS, AND FLATTENING LIDS. ONCE BAKED, PAINT THE TEA SET IN YOUR FAVORITE COLORS AND TEA IS SERVED!

WHAT YOU WILL NEED

- Basic salt-dough recipe (see page 10)
- Basic equipment (see page 8)
- Water-based paints and paintbrush

1 **MAKE SALT-DOUGH** Make the dough following the instructions on page 10. Knead it into a smooth dough, collecting all the bits in the bowl to form a ball.

2 **MAKE TEAPOT** Take a piece of dough, roll it between your hands, and form it into a ball to make the teapot. Roll a small ball from dough and flatten it to make the lid. Put the lid on the pot and add a tiny ball of dough for the lid handle.

3

FINISH TEAPOT Make a handle for the teapot using a small sausage of dough and a spout shape, and stick all the pieces together to make the teapot. Use a little water to stick them together if they are a little dry. Put onto the baking sheet or microwaveable plate.

4

MAKE A CUP Take a piece of dough and form into a cup shape, pressing your fingers or thumb down in the center. Add a small dough handle made from a sausage-shaped piece of dough and put the cup onto the baking sheet or plate.

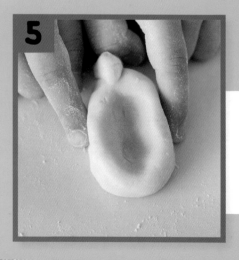

5

MAKE A SMALL MILK JUG Make a smaller cup shape and squash it into a jug shape, adding a handle from a sausage-shaped piece of dough, and put it onto the baking sheet or plate.

6 **BAKE** Bake all the pieces following the instructions on pages 11–12 until they are completely hard. Large pieces will take up to 2 hours in the oven. Leave them in longer if they are still slightly soft. Let cool.

PAINT Paint them in your chosen colors. First, paint the base color, making sure that you cover all the shape. Let them dry completely.

DECORATE When the base color is dry, decorate the tea set with matching patterns—try spots and stripes in different colors. Let them dry completely before you serve tea.

Crafty Tip

Add to your tea set with plates and saucers, cut out with round cutters.

Softy the Snowman

WHEN THERE'S NOT ENOUGH SNOW OUTSIDE, MAKE YOUR OWN SNOWMAN FROM SALT-DOUGH! SOFTY IS A GREAT PROJECT FOR A PLAY DATE, WITH EACH CHILD DECORATING AND PAINTING THEIR OWN SNOWMAN AND GIVING IT A PERSONALITY. SOFTY WOULD ALSO MAKE A GREAT ADDITION TO THE WEATHER SYMBOLS IN THE PROJECT ON PAGE 26.

WHAT YOU WILL NEED

- Basic salt-dough recipe (see page 10)
- Basic equipment (see page 8)
- Wooden skewer
- Water-based paints and paintbrush
- Felt for scarf
- Scissors
- White/PVA glue
- Black pipe cleaners

1 **MAKE SALT-DOUGH** Follow the recipe on page 10 to make a quantity of salt-dough, kneading it to form a ball.

2

MAKE BODY Take two pieces of dough, one a little larger than the other, and roll them between your hands into two balls. Put the smaller ball—the head—on top of the larger one to make the snowman's body.

3

MAKE BUTTONS AND NOSE Roll two small pieces of dough into balls and press them onto the snowman as buttons. Shape another small piece into a nose and press it to the head.

MAKE THE HAT Roll two more small pieces into balls, then flatten them slightly, adding them to the top of the head to make the hat.

 **ADD ARMHOLES** Using a wooden skewer or the end of a paintbrush, make holes for the eyes and at either side of the body so that you can add pipe cleaner arms once the snowman is baked. Place on a baking sheet or microwaveable plate.

6  **BAKE** Bake the snowman following the instructions on pages 11–12, until completely hard. Let cool.

PAINT THE BODY First, paint the body white all over and let dry. Then paint the hat with black paint.

PAINT THE BUTTONS Choose some bright colors to paint the buttons, and then paint the snowman's nose in orange. Let the paint dry.

🖐 **ADD SCARF** Wrap your snowman up in a scarf to keep him nice and warm. Cut a strip of felt and wrap it around his neck, using a dab of glue to keep it in place.

🖐 **ADD ARMS** Cut the pipe cleaners into two short lengths and push them into the holes, bending them a little to make arms. You may need to add a little glue to keep the arms in place.

Gingerbread Family

THE GINGERBREAD MAN IS A CLASSIC STORY THAT LITTLE ONES WILL ENJOY ENACTING WITH THESE CUTE LITTLE FIGURES. USING COOKIE CUTTERS, THEY ARE QUICK AND EASY TO MAKE AND DECORATE, AND CAN BE PAINTED AND DRESSED TO MATCH ANY FAVORITE FAIRYTALE CHARACTER.

WHAT YOU WILL NEED

- Basic salt-dough recipe (see page 10)
- Basic equipment (see page 8)
- Gingerbread family cookie cutters
- Brown water-based paints and paintbrush
- Ricrac braid
- White/PVA glue
- Gems or buttons, scraps of ribbon and braid, to decorate
- Felt for hat
- Scissors
- Marker pens

1 **MAKE THE SALT-DOUGH** Follow the recipe on page 10 to make a quantity of salt-dough, kneading it to form a ball.

2

ROLL OUT THE DOUGH Sprinkle flour onto the work surface and place the ball of dough on top. Roll the dough out with a rolling pin to an even thickness of about ½in. (1cm). Cut out a gingerbread man, woman, and child, and place them on the baking sheet or microwaveable plate.

3 **BAKE** Bake all the pieces following the instructions on pages 11–12 until completely hard. Let cool.

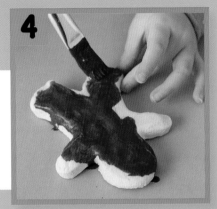

PAINT Use brown paint to paint the gingerbread family all over—start with the front, let dry, then paint the back and sides. Let dry.

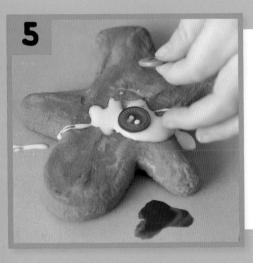

 DECORATE Use dabs of glue to attach gems or buttons to the gingerbread family to decorate their clothes. You could cut pants or a skirt from felt, add hair or a hat—have fun looking through your craft stash for odds and ends to use.

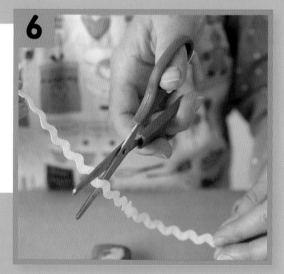

ADD BRAID Glue on strips of ricrac braid or ribbon to add more details.

7

MAKE HAT Cut a square of felt and glue a rectangle of felt to the base for the hat brim, adding a strip of black felt to trim the edge. Glue the hat to your gingerbread man.

8

DRAW FACE Using marker pens, draw the eyes and mouth on your family.

Crafty Tip

CAUTION: Your gingerbread family may look very life-like so make sure your little one doesn't try to take a bite!

These cute figures would also look great as Christmas decorations—simply push a hole through the top before baking (see page 13) and then thread with twine or ribbon to hang on the tree.

Brilliant Beads

WITH A LITTLE ROLLING AND PAINTING, YOUNG CHILDREN WILL SOON MASTER THESE SIMPLE BEADS. PAINTED IN BRIGHT COLORS AND DECORATED WITH GLITTER, GEMS, OR PAINTED DESIGNS, THIS ACTIVITY WILL KEEP LITTLE ONES HAPPILY OCCUPIED FOR AN AFTERNOON.

WHAT YOU WILL NEED

- Basic salt-dough recipe (see page 10)
- Basic equipment (see page 8)
- Wooden skewer
- Short straws (optional)
- Water-based paints and paintbrush
- Sticky gems, glitter, or sequins (optional)
- White/PVA glue (optional)
- Yarn/wool
- Needle

1 **MAKE THE SALT-DOUGH** Follow the recipe on page 10 to make a quantity of salt-dough, kneading it to form a ball.

ROLL BEAD SHAPES Take small pieces of dough and roll them into bead shapes—try round ones, or oval, or squash a round shape to make a cylinder or a cube. Vary the sizes.

2

3

MAKE A HOLE Push a wooden skewer through the center of each bead to make a hole. Make the hole slightly bigger than you need, as it will shrink a little when the salt-dough is baked, or bake with a short straw through the holes (see page 13). Place on a baking sheet or microwaveable plate. Bake until completely hard. Let cool.

PAINT THE BEADS When the beads have cooled completely, paint them in bright colors, making sure they are completely covered in paint. Use a small paintbrush to add some decoration—try spots or stripes. Let them dry.

ADD SOME SPARKLE To make your beads extra special, add a dab of glue and then sprinkle with glitter or add sticky gems.

STRING THE BEADS Cut a length of yarn that is long enough to fit over your child's head and around their neck, adding extra for the knot. Thread the needle with the yarn and help your child to thread the beads in their chosen order.

TIE THE NECKLACE Remove the needle and tie the ends of the necklace with a double knot around your child's neck.

Tic Tac Toe

WITH A LITTLE KNEADING AND ROLLING, THE SIMPLE SHAPES FOR THE GAME OF TIC TAC TOE (ALSO KNOWN AS NOUGHTS AND CROSSES) ARE EASY TO CONSTRUCT. AFTER A LICK OF PAINT, YOU'LL SOON BE BATTLING IT OUT TO FIND THE TIC TAC TOE CHAMPION.

WHAT YOU WILL NEED

- Basic salt-dough recipe (see page 10)
- Basic equipment (see page 8)
- Alphabet cookie cutters (X and O)
- A plate or round object to draw around
- Water-based paints and paintbrush

1 **MAKE THE SALT-DOUGH** Follow the recipe on page 10 to make a quantity of salt-dough, kneading it to form a ball.

2

ROLL OUT THE DOUGH Sprinkle flour onto the work surface and place the ball of dough on top. Roll the dough out with a rolling pin to an even thickness of about ½in. (1cm).

3

CUT SHAPES Using half the dough, cut out 10 round (O) shapes and 10 cross (X) shapes using cookie cutters, and place them on the baking sheet or microwaveable plate.

MAKE THE BASE Take the remaining dough and roll it out as before. Use a plate or other round object as a template and cut a circle from the dough. Using the leftover dough, roll it into four long sausage shapes, to match the diameter of the circle.

MAKE THE GRID Space the rolled "lines" to form a grid pattern on the base, and press them gently to join them to the base.

6 **BAKE** Bake all the pieces following the instructions on pages 11–12 until completely hard. Let cool.

PAINT THE PIECES Use two different colors to paint the noughts and crosses, making sure that you paint them all over. Let dry.

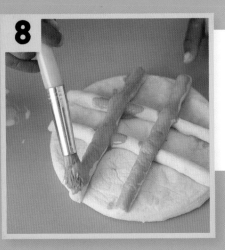

8

PAINT GRID Choose different colors of paint for the base and the grid, painting them all over. Let dry.

ADD VARNISH To make your game more hard-wearing, add a coat of varnish to the pieces when they are dry. Follow the instructions on page 12 to make some varnish, then brush it all over the playing pieces and grid, let dry— then you're ready to play!

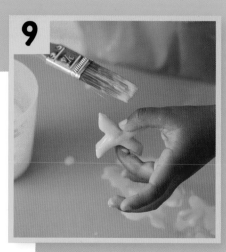

9

Crafty Tip

Don't worry if you don't have alphabet cutters. You can use any shapes to play the game, as long as you have different shapes for each player. Why not try animals, stars, or flowers, instead?

HOW TO PLAY TIC TAC TOE

Decide which player is the "X" and which is the "O." Take it in turns to place your pieces on the grid—the first player to place three pieces in a row is the winner!

Little Ladybug

GO ON A NATURE WALK, OR OUT TO THE BACK YARD, AND SEE WHAT BUGS YOU CAN FIND, THEN RECREATE THEM BACK HOME IN SALT-DOUGH! THIS LITTLE LADYBUG COULD BE THE START OF A COLLECTION—TRY MAKING A BEE, DRAGONFLY, BUTTERFLY, OR EVEN A SPIDER! WE'VE SHOWN YOU HOW TO MAKE A CATERPILLAR COMPANION ON PAGE 74.

WHAT YOU WILL NEED

- Basic salt-dough recipe (see page 10)
- Basic equipment (see page 8)
- Ruler
- Wooden skewer
- Water-based paints and paintbrush
- White/PVA glue
- Googly eyes
- Green pipe cleaners

1 **MAKE THE SALT-DOUGH** Follow the recipe on page 10 to make a quantity of salt-dough, kneading it to form a ball.

2

MAKE THE BODY Take two pieces of dough, one a little larger than the other, and roll them into balls between your hands. Press them together to make the body and head.

3

MAKE THE WINGS Roll another ball of dough and flatten it with your hand into a disc. Use the side of a ruler to cut the disc in half, to give you wings. Gently press the wings onto the body.

MAKE SPOTS Roll small pieces of dough into little balls to make the ladybug's spots. You can make them symmetrical with an even number, such as eight, or uneven—this is a great way to practice some simple math! Squash the balls slightly to flatten them and then stick to the wings.

 MAKE HOLES Use a wooden skewer or the end of a paintbrush to make holes on either side of the head to insert the antennae once the ladybug is baked. Place on a baking sheet or microwaveable plate.

6 **BAKE** Bake your ladybug following the instructions on pages 11–12 until completely hard. Let cool.

PAINT Start by painting the body and wings red, let dry, then paint the head and spots in black. Let dry.

8

STICK ON EYES Use a dab of glue to add the googly eyes to the head.

ADD ANTENNAE Cut two short lengths of green pipe cleaner for the antennae, and push them into the holes. You can add a little glue to help secure them in place.

9

Crafty Tip

The ladybug would look great outdoors in a herb or flower garden—simply mix up some varnish (see page 12), to protect her a little from the elements.

Fairy Toadstools

ENCOURAGE IMAGINATIVE PLAY WITH THESE MAGICAL TOADSTOOLS—PERFECT FOR FAIRIES TO INHABIT OR TO MAKE A FANTASY LANDSCAPE WHERE DINOSAURS OR GIANT INSECTS ROAM! YOUR CHILD WILL ENJOY MODELING THE SHAPES AND ADDING THE FINISHING TOUCHES.

WHAT YOU WILL NEED

- Basic salt-dough recipe (see page 10)
- Basic equipment (see page 8)
- Round cookie cutters
- Water-based paints and paintbrush
- White/PVA glue
- Mini craft pompoms

1 **MAKE THE SALT-DOUGH** Follow the recipe on page 10 to make a quantity of salt-dough, kneading it to form a ball.

2

ROLL OUT THE DOUGH Sprinkle flour onto the work surface and place the ball of dough on top. Roll the dough out with a rolling pin to an even thickness of about ½in. (1cm).

3

CUT OUT CIRCLES Using round cookie cutters, cut out circles from the dough for the tops of the toadstools—we made one large and one small. Put to one side on some baking parchment.

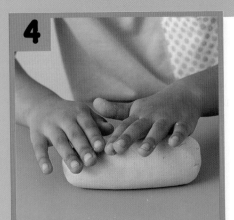

4

MAKE STALKS Roll fat, short shapes for the stalks. Press the stalk to the underside of the circle (so that the toadstool is upside down) and transfer to the baking sheet or microwaveable plate.

MAKE GRASS For the grass base, roll a fat oblong shape and squash it lightly to flatten it. Place upside down on the baking sheet or microwaveable plate so that they hold their shape.

5

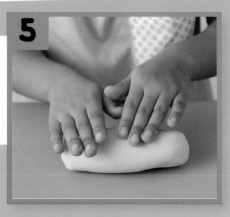

6 **BAKE** Bake the pieces following the instructions on pages 11–12 until completely hard. Let cool.

BAKE Bake your toadstool tops red and the grass green. We left our stalks unpainted as the baked dough looks very realistic. Let dry.

7

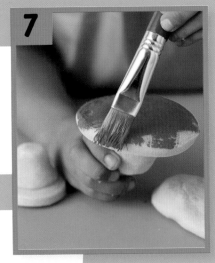

8 **GLUE** the toadstools to the grass base, holding them in place while the glue sets.

9

DECORATE Have fun adding pompom spots to the top of your toadstools!

Crafty Tip

Make a woodland scene by adding little ladybugs (see page 46) and caterpillars (see page 74).

Pretty Flower Brooch

THIS PRETTY BROOCH IS A VARIATION ON THE SHERIFF'S BADGE ON PAGE 28, BUT MADE WITH FLOWER CUTTERS AND PAINTED IN SOFT PASTEL COLORS—PERFECT FOR A MOTHER'S DAY GIFT.

WHAT YOU WILL NEED

- Basic salt-dough recipe (see page 10)
- Basic equipment (see page 8)
- Round, fluted, and flower shape cookie cutters
- Water-based paints and paintbrush
- White/PVA glue
- Button
- Scrap of fabric
- Scissors
- Safety pin

1 **MAKE THE SALT-DOUGH** Follow the recipe on page 10 to make a quantity of salt-dough, kneading it to form a ball.

2

ROLL OUT THE DOUGH Sprinkle some flour onto the work surface and roll out the dough to a thickness of about ¼in. (5mm) using the rolling pin. Sprinkle flour onto the dough to prevent it getting too sticky.

3

CUT OUT THE SHAPES Using the shaped cookie cutters, cut out a large circle, a smaller circle with a fluted edge, and a flower shape. Lay them on a baking sheet or microwaveable plate.

4 **BAKE AND PAINT** Bake the shapes following the instructions on pages 11–12 until completely hard. When the pieces have all cooled, paint them in soft pastel colors, or bright colors if you like, making sure you have covered the front and back thoroughly, and let them dry.

GLUE TOGETHER Using white/PVA glue, stick the three parts of the brooch together, with the large circle as the base, the fluted circle in the middle, and the flower shape on top. Glue a little button in the center. Let it dry.

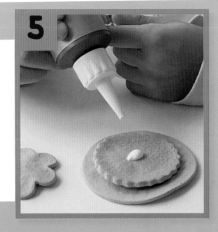

ADD BACK Cut a small piece of fabric and thread it through a safety pin. Glue the fabric onto the back of the brooch and let it dry completely.

Fun Fruit

MAKING PLAY FOOD IS A GREAT WAY TO EXTEND IMAGINATIVE PLAY, BUT MAKE SURE YOUR CHILD DOESN'T ATTEMPT TO EAT ANY. CHILDREN CAN CHOOSE THEIR FAVORITE FRUITS, ADDING TO THE FRUIT BOWL AS THEY GO. YOU CAN, OF COURSE, EXTEND THE ACTIVITY TO MAKE VEGETABLES, PIZZA, ICE CREAM, CUPCAKES ...

WHAT YOU WILL NEED

- Basic salt-dough recipe (see page 10)
- Basic equipment (see page 8)
- Stick or skewer
- Water-based paints and paintbrush
- Green pipe cleaner
- White/PVA glue
- Scissors
- Green felt (optional)

1 **MAKE THE SALT-DOUGH** Follow the recipe on page 10 to make a quantity of salt-dough, mixing it to form a firm dough.

TO MAKE THE STRAWBERRY

MAKE A STRAWBERRY Take a piece of dough, roll it, and form it into a strawberry shape (a little like a heart shape), squashing and molding it with your fingers.

3 **ADD SEEDS** Use the end of a wooden skewer to press little indents into the strawberry to make the seeds.

4

MAKE A LEAF Take a small piece of dough and roll and shape it into a leaf shape, then carefully stick it to the top of the strawberry. Add three leaves to each strawberry.

TO MAKE THE CHERRIES AND GRAPES

5

ROLL CHERRIES AND GRAPES Make cherries and grapes from small balls of dough, rolling them in your hands or on the work surface to make round shapes.

ADD A HOLE Make a slight hole in the top of the cherries with a wooden skewer, so that the pipe cleaner stalks can be pushed in place when the fruits have been baked. Put the grapes together to make a bunch.

6

7 **BAKE THE FRUIT SHAPES** Place the fruit on a baking sheet or microwaveable plate. Bake following the instructions on pages 11–12 until completely hard. Let cool.

8

PAINT Paint the strawberries red and their leaves green, the grapes pale green, and the cherries dark red, making sure that the whole surface is covered. Let them dry.

9

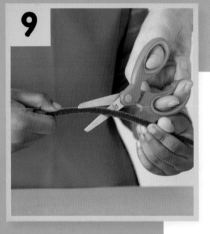

ADD STALKS Cut a length of green pipe cleaner and bend it in half. Glue each end into the cherries. You could add a stalk to the bunch of grapes, too.

10

ADD LEAVES To give your cherries a finishing touch, you could cut a small leaf shape from felt and glue it to the center of the stalk.

ADD VARNISH When all the pieces are dry, paint them with a coat of varnish (see page 12) to make them slightly shiny and protect their surfaces from chipping.

Handprint Tile

SALT-DOUGH IS A GREAT WAY TO PRESERVE LITTLE HANDPRINTS, OR FOOTPRINTS. CHILDREN WILL LOVE THE IDEA OF IMPRINTING THEIR HAND, AND YOU CAN ALSO COMBINE IT WITH HANDPRINTS OF BABY SIBLINGS, TOO— PERFECT AS A GIFT FOR GRANDPARENTS.

WHAT YOU WILL NEED

- Basic salt-dough recipe (see page 10)
- Basic equipment (see page 8)
- Wooden skewer
- Water-based paint and paintbrush

1 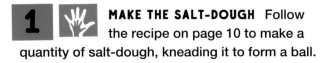 **MAKE THE SALT-DOUGH** Follow the recipe on page 10 to make a quantity of salt-dough, kneading it to form a ball.

ROLL OUT THE DOUGH Sprinkle flour onto the work surface and place the ball of dough on top. Roll the dough out with a rolling pin to an even thickness of about 1in. (2.5cm). Cut or shape the dough into a circle, oval, square, or rectangle—whatever shape you would like for the tile.

MAKE PRINT Hold your child's arm and guide his or her outstretched hand flat onto the salt-dough. Hold in place and press gently, then lift the hand straight up to leave a clear imprint. Older children can make the print themselves but take care not to press too hard.

4

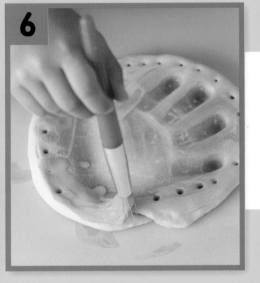

6

ADD PATTERN If you like, you can decorate the tile before it is baked. Draw a pattern in the dough with a wooden skewer or the end of a paintbrush. Place on a baking sheet or microwaveable plate.

5 **BAKE** Bake the tile following the instructions on pages 11–12 until completely hard. Let cool.

PAINT Now add some pretty colors to your tile. Paint the background, then let it dry before painting the handprint a different color to make it stand out.

Dotty Dino

THIS CUTE LITTLE CHARACTER IS VERY EASY TO MAKE AND IS A GREAT TOY FOR IMAGINATIVE PLAY OR STORY-TELLING. MAKE LOTS OF DINOSAURS AT THE SAME TIME, OR COMBINE THIS PROJECT WITH OTHERS USING COOKIE CUTTERS (SEE PAGES 64 AND 67) TO CREATE A WHOLE MENAGERIE OF SALT-DOUGH CREATURES!

WHAT YOU WILL NEED

- Basic salt-dough recipe (see page 10)
- Basic equipment (see page 8)
- Dinosaur cookie cutter
- Water-based paints and paintbrush
- White/PVA glue
- Googly eyes

1

MAKE THE SALT-DOUGH Follow the recipe on page 10 to make a quantity of salt-dough, kneading it to form a ball.

2

ROLL OUT THE DOUGH Sprinkle flour onto the work surface and place the ball of dough on top. Roll the dough out with a rolling pin to an even thickness of about ½in. (1cm).

3

CUT OUT SHAPE Dip the cookie cutter in flour, then press into the dough to cut out a dinosaur. Cut out as many dinosaurs or shapes as you need.

ROLL DOTS Take small pieces of dough and roll them between your fingers to make small balls. Squash the balls a little and then push them onto the dinosaur's body. Place on a baking sheet or microwaveable plate.

 5 **BAKE** Bake the dinosaur following the instructions on pages 11–12 until completely hard. Let cool.

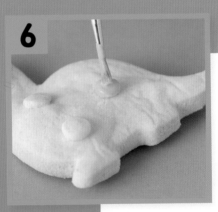

PAINT Choose a color and paint the dots, then paint the dinosaur's body in a contrasting color. Remember to paint the back, too. Let dry.

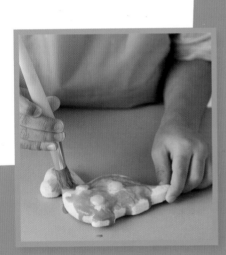

ADD EYES Glue a googly eye to your dinosaur to finish. Make some more!

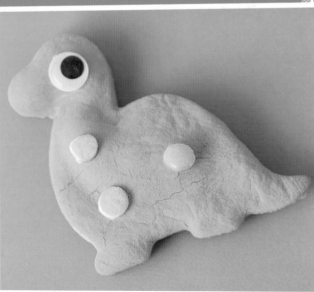

Trinket Pot

SALT-DOUGH IS SOFT AND TACTILE, WHICH MAKES IT A LOVELY MATERIAL TO USE FOR MOLDING AND MODELING. THIS LITTLE POT IS IDEAL FOR SMALL HANDS TO CREATE, AND WE'VE MADE OURS FROM COLORED DOUGH, WHICH ADDS ANOTHER FUN ELEMENT WHEN KNEADING AND SHAPING. ONCE BAKED, THE TRINKET POT IS PERFECT FOR STORING ALL THOSE TINY BITS AND PIECES THAT ACCUMULATE FROM NOWHERE!

WHAT YOU WILL NEED

- Basic salt-dough recipe (see page 10)
- Basic equipment (see page 8)
- Water-based paints and paintbrush
- White/PVA glue
- Button to decorate

 COLOR THE SALT-DOUGH Follow the recipe on page 10 to make a quantity of salt-dough, kneading it to form a ball. Separate the dough into three pieces and follow the instructions on page 11 to color the dough with different colors of paint; we used pink, blue, and green.

MAKE THE POT Take a ball of pink dough for the base and mold and shape it into a small pot, pushing down in the center and shaping the edges.

MAKE THE RIM Take a piece of blue dough and roll it into a long sausage that will fit the circumference of the pot. Press it gently around the rim of the pot, curving it round. Put on a baking sheet or microwaveable plate.

MAKE THE LID Using your third color of dough, roll a small ball between your hands and then flatten it slightly to make a disc. Check that the disc is large enough to cover the top of the pot.

DECORATE LID Use little pieces of dough to decorate the lid. Put on the baking sheet or microwaveable plate.

BAKE Bake the pieces following the instructions on pages 11–12 until completely hard. Leave to cool.

FINISHING TOUCH To give your trinket pot a finishing touch, glue a pretty button to the lid, or you could use a gem for something sparkly!

Hanging Butterflies

THESE PRETTY BUTTERFLIES MAKE THE PERFECT DECORATION FOR A LITTLE GIRL'S ROOM. YOU CAN ADAPT THEM TO MATCH ANY COLOR SCHEME, AND THERE'S LOTS OF OPPORTUNITY TO DECORATE THEM IN DIFFERENT WAYS.

WHAT YOU WILL NEED

- Basic salt-dough recipe (see page 10)
- Basic equipment (see page 8)
- Butterfly cookie cutters
- Wooden skewer
- Short drinking straws (optional)
- Water-based paints and paintbrush
- White/PVA glue
- Gems or sequins
- Marker pens
- Ribbon

1 **MAKE THE SALT-DOUGH** Follow the recipe on page 10 to make a quantity of salt-dough, kneading it to form a ball.

ROLL OUT THE DOUGH Sprinkle flour onto the work surface and place the ball of dough on top. Roll the dough out with a rolling pin to an even thickness of about ½in. (1cm). Dip the cookie cutter in flour and cut out as many butterflies as you need. Place on the baking sheet or microwaveable plate.

Crafty Tip

Instead of painting the butterflies, color the dough (see page 11) before baking, then simply decorate!

3

ADD HOLES Use a wooden skewer or the end of a paintbrush to make two holes in the center of the butterfly's body, to thread through the ribbon. Placing a short drinking straw in each hole will help to keep them open during baking (see page 13).

4 **BAKE** Bake the butterflies following the instructions on pages 11–12 and let harden completely.

5

PAINT When the butterflies are cool and dry, paint them in pretty colors so that they are covered on all sides, back, and front, and let dry completely.

6

DECORATE Give your butterflies patterned wings by gluing on sparkly gems or sequins, or draw patterns with marker pens or paint.

7

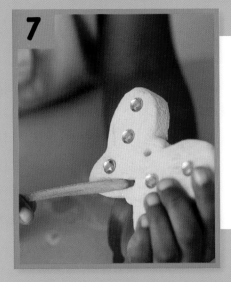

THREAD RIBBON To display the butterflies, thread the ribbon through the holes, knotting it at the top and bottom of each butterfly and spacing them at regular intervals.

Crafty Tip

Try this idea with fish or shark shapes to make an under-the-sea theme.

Fishing Game

ONCE YOUR CHILD HAS CUT OUT THE FISH AND PAINTED THEM IN BRIGHT, TROPICAL COLORS, THERE'S EVEN MORE FUN TO BE HAD TRYING TO CATCH THEM! THIS FISHING GAME IS A GREAT ACTIVITY FOR COORDINATION AND FINE MOTOR SKILLS—KEEP IT SIMPLE WITH JUST THE FISHING RODS, OR MAKE A WHOLE UNDERWATER SCENE BY DECORATING AN OLD BOX TO CAST INTO.

WHAT YOU WILL NEED

- Basic salt-dough recipe (see page 10)
- Basic equipment (see page 8)
- Fish cookie cutter
- Water-based paints and paintbrush
- Wooden skewer
- Paperclips
- Twine/string or yarn
- Short garden cane (optional)
- Colored duct tape (optional)

1 **MAKE THE SALT-DOUGH** Follow the recipe on page 10 to make a quantity of salt-dough, kneading it to form a ball.

ROLL OUT THE DOUGH Sprinkle flour onto the work surface and place the ball of dough on top. Roll the dough out with a rolling pin to an even thickness of about ½in. (1cm). Dip the cookie cutter in flour and cut out as many fish as you need—four or five will make a good game—then place on the baking sheet or microwaveable plate.

ADD HOLES Use the end of a wooden skewer or a paintbrush to a make hole at the top of the body. Make sure the hole is quite close to the edge of the body so that you can thread through the paperclip. Placing a short drinking straw in the holes will help to keep them open during baking (see page 13).

4 **BAKE** Bake the fish shapes following the instructions on pages 11–12 until completely hard. Let cool.

5

PAINT Use bright colors to paint the fish, making sure that you cover them all over, back and front. You could add patterns or embellishments to make them even more exotic. Let dry.

 ADD VARNISH To strengthen your fish and make them more hard-wearing, apply a layer of varnish, following the instructions on page 12.

6

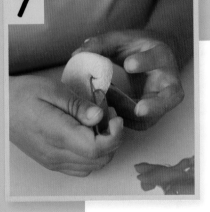

7

THREAD PAPERCLIP Unbend the end of a paperclip and feed it through the hole in the fish, then bend it back to secure it in place. Repeat for all the fish.

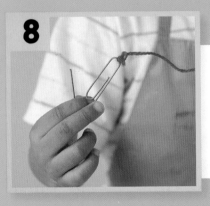

8

 ATTACH HOOK Knot a length of twine or yarn through another paperclip and open out the end to make a hook. You're ready to go fishing!

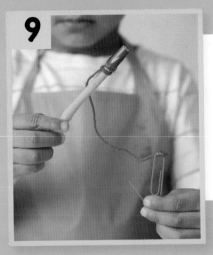

MAKE FISHING ROD If you'd like to make a proper fishing rod, attach the twine to the end of a garden cane using colored duct tape. You could also paint the cane if you like, making canes in different colors for each player.

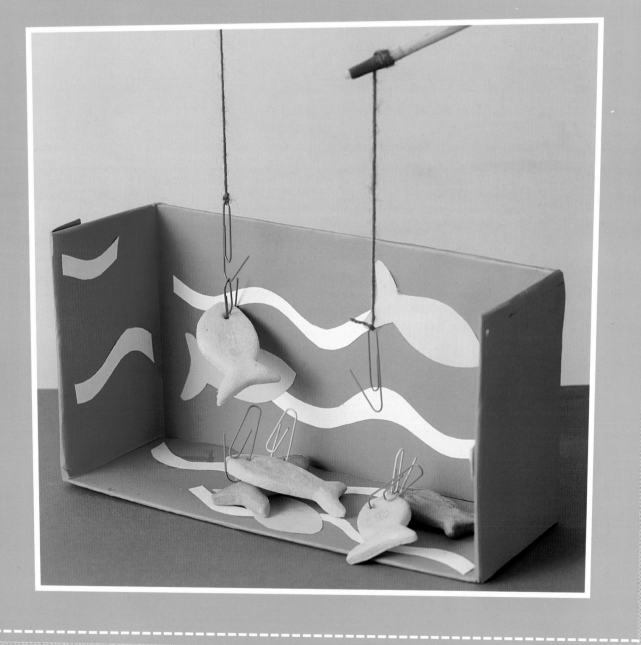

Springtime Eggs

WHAT YOU WILL NEED

- Basic salt-dough recipe (see page 10)
- Basic equipment (see page 8)
- Water-based paints
- White/PVA glue
- Ribbon, ricrac, craft feathers, buttons, pompoms, to decorate

COLORED SALT-DOUGH PRODUCES VERY PRETTY PASTEL SHADES THAT ARE PERFECT FOR MAKING SPRINGTIME DECORATIONS. MOLDING THE DOUGH INTO AN EGG SHAPE IS LOTS OF FUN AND ONCE BAKED, YOUR CHILD CAN ADD ALL KINDS OF DECORATIONS TO MAKE THEM EXTRA SPECIAL.

COLOR THE SALT-DOUGH Follow the recipe on page 10 to make a quantity of salt-dough, kneading it to form a ball. Separate the dough and follow the instructions on page 11 to color the dough with different pastel colors—we made green, pink, purple, blue, and yellow.

SHAPE THE EGG Take a piece of colored dough and roll it into a ball, then mold the ball into an egg shape. Place on a baking sheet or microwaveable plate as you work. Make more eggs in different colors.

3  **BAKE** Bake your eggs following the instructions on pages 11–12, until they have hardened completely. Let cool.

4

DECORATE Have fun decorating your eggs with pretty craft embellishments, gluing them on to the baked egg.

5

DISPLAY You'll want to display your eggs when they are finished—add them to an egg carton or spring basket for the Easter bunny to deliver.

Crafty Tip

Make the eggs slightly smaller than they need to be as they may expand when baked, and bear in mind that the back of the egg may flatten and spread a little, too.

Lovely Letters

MADE WITH ALPHABET COOKIE CUTTERS, THESE LETTERS ARE PERFECT FOR CHILDREN TO MAKE WITH MINIMAL SUPERVISION, AND MAXIMUM CREATIVITY. FROM A DECORATIVE ALPHABET TO DISPLAY ON A SHELF OR ATTACH TO THE FRIDGE, TO NAMES AND NEW WORDS, THERE'S ENDLESS SCOPE FOR FUN AND LEARNING.

WHAT YOU WILL NEED

- Basic salt-dough recipe (see page 10)
- Basic equipment (see page 8)
- Alphabet cookie cutters
- Water-based paints and paintbrush
- White/PVA glue
- Craft embellishments (optional)
- Small magnet (optional)

1 **MAKE THE SALT-DOUGH** Follow the recipe on page 10 to make a quantity of salt-dough, kneading it to form a ball.

ROLL OUT THE DOUGH Sprinkle flour onto the work surface and place the ball of dough on top. Roll the dough out with a rolling pin to an even thickness of about ½in. (1cm).

CUT OUT LETTERS Use the cutters to cut out the letters and place them onto the baking sheet or microwaveable plate. Bake the letters following the instructions on pages 11–12 until completely hard. Let cool.

PAINT THE LETTERS Paint the letters in a variety of bright colors. Paint the whole surface of the letter, back and front and along the edges, so that the surface is completely covered. Let dry.

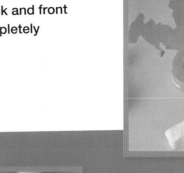

4

5

DECORATE When the base coat is dry, add patterns in another color of paint, or stick on craft embellishments such as gems, sequins, beads, feathers, or pompoms.

6

ADD MAGNET If you'd like to display your letters on the fridge or a magnetic board, glue a small magnet to the back of the letter. Let the glue dry.

Crafty Tip

This is a fun activity for a crafty party—everyone can take their magnetic initial or name home as a party favor at the end of the day.

Cute Caterpillar

THIS LITTLE CATERPILLAR MODEL IS HAPPILY AT HOME ON A LEAF, ABOUT TO START MUNCHING! WITH SOME SIMPLE SHAPING AND ROLLING, HE IS VERY QUICK TO CONSTRUCT AND THEN YOU CAN MAKE HIM AS EXOTIC AS YOU LIKE WITH BRIGHT AND COLORFUL PAINT.

WHAT YOU WILL NEED

- Basic salt-dough recipe (see page 10)
- Basic equipment
- Blunt knife
- Wooden skewer
- Water-based paints and paintbrush
- Black pipe cleaners
- Scissors
- White/PVA glue

1 **MAKE THE SALT-DOUGH** Follow the recipe on page 10 to make a quantity of salt-dough, kneading it to form a ball.

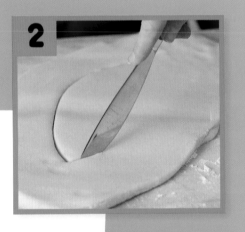

ROLL OUT DOUGH Sprinkle flour onto the work surface and place the ball of dough on top. Roll the dough out with a rolling pin to an even thickness of about ½in. (1cm). Use a blunt knife to cut out a leaf shape.

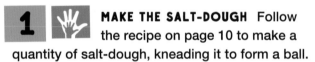

MARK LEAF Add the leaf veins using a wooden skewer or the end of a paintbrush. Put to one side on the baking sheet or microwaveable plate.

ROLL Take small pieces of dough and roll them into balls between your hands; make one large ball for the head and then five small balls for the body.

MAKE BODY Assemble the body on top of the leaf by pressing the balls together to make the sections of the body and head. Roll some tiny balls for eyes and push them onto the head.

 **MAKE HOLES** Use a wooden skewer or the end of a paintbrush to make holes on either side of the head to insert the antennae once baked.

7  **BAKE** Bake your caterpillar and leaf following the instructions on pages 11–12 until completely hard. Let cool.

8

PAINT Start by painting the leaf green, then paint the head, eyes, and body in different colors. Let dry.

9

ADD ANTENNAE Cut two short lengths of black pipe cleaner for the antennae, and push them into the holes. You can add a little glue to help secure them in place if necessary.

Pretty Pendant

THIS PROJECT MAKES A LOVELY GIFT FOR A FRIEND, OR THE PERFECT PARTY ACTIVITY WHERE EVERYONE GETS TO TAKE THEIR NECKLACE HOME AS A PARTY FAVOR AT THE END.

WHAT YOU WILL NEED

- Basic salt-dough recipe (see page 10)
- Basic equipment (see page 8)
- Heart cookie cutters
- Wooden skewer (optional)
- Water-based paint and paintbrush
- White/PVA glue
- Glitter
- Ribbon

1 **MAKE THE SALT-DOUGH** Follow the recipe on page 10 to make a quantity of salt-dough, kneading it to form a ball.

2

ROLL OUT THE DOUGH Sprinkle flour onto the work surface and place the ball of dough on top. Roll the dough out with a rolling pin to an even thickness of about ½in. (1cm). Dip the cookie cutters in flour and cut out a large and small heart. Place on the baking sheet or microwaveable plate.

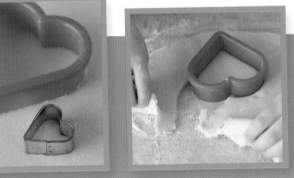

3

ADD HOLE Use a wooden skewer or the end of a paintbrush to make a hole in the top of the large heart, to thread through the ribbon.

4  **BAKE** Bake the hearts following the instructions on pages 11–12 until completely hard. Let cool.

PAINT When the hearts are cool and dry, paint them so that they are covered on all sides, back, and front, and let dry completely. Paint the smaller heart a different color, if you like.

GLUE TOGETHER Add a dab of glue to the back of the small heart and stick it to the center of the large heart. Let dry.

7 **ADD SPARKLE** Put a few dabs of glue all over the heart and then sprinkle with glitter. Shake off the excess and return it to the glitter pot. Let the glue dry.

ADD RIBBON Thread a length of ribbon through the hole and then tie the ends in a knot to secure.

Suppliers

US

A C Moore
www.acmoore.com

Create for Less
www.createforless.com

The Cookie Cutter Company
www.cookiecuttercompany.com

Darice
www.darice.com

Fancy Flours
www.fancyflours.com

Hobby Lobby
www.hobbylobby.com

Jo-ann Fabric & Crafts
www.joann.com

Michaels
www.michaels.com

Mister Art
www.misterart.com

Walmart
www.walmart.com

UK

Baker Ross
www.bakerross.co.uk

Cakes Cookies and Crafts
www.cakescookiesandcraftsshop.co.uk

Early Learning Centre
www.elc.co.uk

Homecrafts Direct
www.homecrafts.co.uk

Hobbycraft
www.hobbycraft.co.uk

John Lewis
www.johnlewis.co.uk

Lakeland
www.lakeland.co.uk

Mulberry Bush
www.mulberrybush.co.uk

The Works
www.theworks.co.uk

Yellow Moon
www.yellowmoon.org.uk

CREDITS

Photography by Terry Benson, except for the flower brooch, pages 52–53, by Debbie Patterson

Styling by Emily Breen, except for the flower brooch, pages 52–53, by Emma Hardy

Projects devised by Katie Hardwicke and Emily Breen except for:

Emma Hardy: letters, tea set, beads, fruit, flower brooch and sheriff's badge

Linda Collister: Gingerbread family

CICO Books would like to thank Megan Breen for the loan of her toys.

Index

Bb
badge, sheriff's 28–30
beads 40–41
brooch, flower 52–53
butterflies, hanging 64–66

Cc
caterpillar 74–76
cherries 55–57
Christmas decorations
  gingerbread figures 39
  snowman 34–36
  twinkly stars 19–21
clearing up 9
clothing 9
cloud 27
colored salt-dough 11
cookie cutters
  butterflies 64–66
  dinosaur 60–61
  fish 64, 67–69
  flower brooch 52–53
  gingerbread family 37–39
  letters 42–45, 72–73
  pendant 77–79
  sheriff's badge 28–30
  stamped magnets 17
  tic tac toe 42–45
  toadstools 49
  twinkly stars 19–21
  using 13
craft materials 8
cup 32
cutting dough 13, 24

Dd
dinosaur 60–61
donuts 14–15

Ee
eggs, Springtime 70–71
equipment 8, 9, 80

Ff
figures
  butterflies 64–66
  caterpillar 74–76
  dinosaur 60–61
  fish 64, 67–69
  fluffy sheep 22–23
  gingerbread family 37–39
  ladybug 46–48
  snowman 34–36

fish
  fishing game 67–69
  hanging 64
flower brooch 52–53
fruit 54–57

Gg
games
  fishing 67–69
  tic tac toe 42–45
gingerbread family 37–39
glitter, using 9
glue, PVA 12
grapes 55–57

Hh
handprint tiles 58–59
heart pendant 77–79
holes
  making 13, 20
  patterns 25, 54, 59

Ii
insects
  butterfly 65–66
  caterpillar 74–76
  ladybug 46–48

Jj
jewelry
  flower brooch 52–53
  necklace 40–41, 77–79
jug 32

Ll
ladybug 46–48
letters 42–45, 72–73

Mm
magnets
  letters 73
  stamped 16–18
materials 8, 80
mess, preventing 9
microwave, baking dough 12
molded shapes
  beads 40–41
  caterpillar 74–76
  donuts 14–15
  eggs 70–71
  fruit 54–57

ladybug 46–48
sheep 22–23
snowman 34–36
tea set 31–33
toadstools 49–51
trinket pot 62–63
weather symbols 26–27, 34
motor skills 6, 67

Nn
necklaces 40–41, 77–79
noughts and crosses 42–45

Oo
oven, baking dough 11

Pp
paintbrushes, cleaning 9
party favors 73, 77
patterns
  embossed 25, 59, 63, 65, 71, 73
  holes 25, 54, 59
  scored 25
  stamped 16–18, 58–59
pendant heart 77–79
plates 33
pots
  tea pot 31–33
  trinket pot 62–63
preparation 9

Rr
rainbow 27
rolling out 13

Ss
salt-dough
  cutting 13, 24
  making 10–11
  making holes 13, 20
  microwave baking 12
  oven baking 11
  rolling out 13
  unused dough 13
sharks, hanging 64
sheep, fluffy 22–23
sheriff's badge 28–30
snowman 34–36
stamped items
  handprint tiles 58–59
  magnets 16–18

stars
  sheriff's badge 28–30
  twinkly 19–21
strawberry 54–57
sun 27
supervision 6
surfaces
  dusting with flour 13
  protecting 9

Tt
tea set 31–33
tic tac toe 42–45
tiles
  handprint 58–59
  patterned 24–25
toadstools 49–51
trinket pot 62–63

Uu
unused dough 13

Vv
varnish, making 12

Ww
weather symbols 26–27, 34